Borderless Banking
Exploring Cross-Border Payments Through Blockchain

Table of Contents

Chapter 1. Introduction

Diving into the heart of modern financial transactions, our Special Report - "Borderless Banking: Exploring Cross-Border Payments Through Blockchain" - offers comprehensive insight into a world where boundaries are becoming a thing of the past. This highly technical yet intriguing topic is unpacked in a way that is not only accessible, but also enthralling, helping even the most novice reader grasp the complex interplay between international banking, blockchain technology and the revolution in cross-border payments. While we've ensured to handle this delicate subject with the gravity and meticulousness it requires, we also take you on an exciting journey across this new horizon. This report promises to be an invaluable resource and a captivating read that could well illuminate the path for your next investment decision, arming you with vital knowledge. Delve in, and unveil the future of money transfer, today.

Chapter 2. The Advent of Borderless Banking

In the past, banks and financial institutions were brick-and-mortar entities. Banking transactions would occur in one nation and within a single particular community. Fast forward to today, and we find ourselves in an era where geographical boundaries are losing their hold on financial transactions. This phenomenon is not a sudden burst, but the gradual evolution of banking and money transfers, being shaped by numerous driving forces.

2.1. Technological Advancement & Internet

With technology and the internet penetrating almost every facet of human life, the banking sector is certainly not left out. The adoption of information technology in banking happened in four distinct phases. Initially, computers used to handle accounting and record-keeping tasks, replicating manual processes on machines. The second phase saw the introduction of connected networks, enabling inter-branch connections, ATMs, phone and internet banking. The third phase was baked with e-banking initiatives, while the fourth ushered in the era of 'convergence', implementing technology-driven products and services like online bill paying, digital wallets, and more.

2.2. Erosion of Physical Boundaries

As banks began to leverage the internet, physical and geographical boundaries gradually started to erode. Banking transactions that would previously have taken days to process could now be executed in mere minutes. Money transfers were no longer tied down to the local bank's operating hours. Customers could access their bank accounts from anywhere in the world, perform transactions, apply for loans, or even open new accounts.

2.3. Legislation and Regulation

Regulations played a significant role in shaping the advent of borderless banking. Countries and zones began evolving policies to form the foundations of a borderless financial world. These regulations allowed for banking transactions to be performed beyond country borders, encouraging banks to go international. Cross-border payments then got faster, more comfortable, and more reliable. For example, the SEPA (the Single Euro Payment Area) formed by European countries made Euro transfers between European countries as easy as domestic payments.

2.4. Advent of Blockchain & Cryptocurrency

Blockchain technology took the financial world by storm by introducing cryptocurrencies like Bitcoin. Cryptocurrency works on the decentralized blockchain, which grants solid security, reducing the need for intermediaries, and focuses more on peer-to-peer transactions. This technology fundamentally transforms the way cross-border payments function. It impedes double-spending, fast-tracks international transfers, cuts down costs, and offers unparalleled transparency. Cryptocurrencies are indifferent to geographical and political borders, embodying the essence of borderless banking.

2.5. Banks and Financial Institutions' Adaptation

Recognizing the potential of borderless transactions, banks and financial institutions are continuously integrating technology with their core banking platforms. Fintech firms are playing a substantial role in this transformation. In collaboration with banks, they're developing innovative products to ease cross-border payments. Banks are transitioning from being traditional entities to becoming digital ecosystems that leverage data, advanced analytics, and cognitive computing. Furthermore, companies like Ripple are working with banks, simplifying the global payment system and unlocking the true power of blockchain.

This transformation into a borderless world of finance is not without its challenges. From managing legal and regulatory hurdles across various geographies to addressing cybersecurity concerns and ensuring seamless service regardless of bandwidth limitations, the path isn't necessarily smooth. However, the continued advancements and integrations in this realm speak volumes about where we are headed. As borderless banking evolves and matures, the lines governing territorial financial control continue to blur, making money truly global.

The advent of borderless banking is a dance between the old and new. It is a delicate ballet of coexistence and collaboration between traditional banking methods and revolutionary technologies that circumvent geographical boundaries and outdated protocols. It is the beginning of a new world order characterized by unrestricted, transparent, and instantaneous financial transactions, mirroring the rapidly globalizing world we live in. Overall, this evolution increases the accessibility and democratisation of financial services which are central to the world's economic growth and financial inclusion.

Chapter 3. Blockchain Unraveled: A Simple Guide

Blockchain technology is revolutionizing industries, significantly impacting the way we conduct financial transactions. In the realm of international banking, it plays a pivotal role specifically in cross-border payments. Before we explore this aspect more deeply, it's crucial that we gain a thorough understanding of what blockchain technology is, and how it works.

3.1. Fundamentals of Blockchain

Blockchain, as its name suggests, is quite literally a chain of blocks; and no, we aren't talking about the kinds of blocks you played with as a child – these are digital blocks. Each block is a record of transactions. Once a block is filled up with transactions, it is then added to the chain, thus forming a solid block of data. When you hear people talking about a "decentralized, distributed ledger," this chain is what they're referring to.

The earliest block, known as the genesis block, is a unique block. It is the only block that will not point back to a previous block because, when the blockchain was initially designed, there was no previous block. Every block that follows it, however, is regular and, as such, each contains a hash — a special code that allows the block to reference a previous block.

This connection between blocks - the reference through hash codes, forms a chain of blocks, hence the term "blockchain." The chain is continuingly updated, so every ledger in the network is the same, giving each member the ability to prove who owns what at any given time.

3.2. Blockchain and Encryption

Blockchain employs the principles of cryptography to provide its distinctive feature — immutability. Each block contains a cryptographic hash of the previous block, transaction data, and a timestamp. The hash is a complex algorithm that transforms any amount of text into a fixed series of characters. Everyone can see these sequences, but the information they contain is secure. This is how the immutability of the blockchain is achieved.

The hash ensures that every block is unique, and every block's cryptographic reference to the previous block creates a chain. If someone tries to alter a transaction or block, the blockchain changes the hash. However, it's nearly impossible to achieve without being noticed because other blocks in the chain store the original hash.

3.3. Decentralization: A Key Feature

One of the hallmarks of blockchain technology is its decentralized nature. Here, decentralization refers to the idea that instead of being held on one server and regulated by a single entity (like a bank or government), multiple copies of the blockchain are held by multiple parties (nodes), forming a decentralized network of ledgers. Each node has a full copy of the data.

Decentralization is fundamentally what keeps the blockchain secure. Because each node is constantly checking its version of the blockchain against those of the other nodes, it is extremely difficult for anyone to cheat the system. This leads to increased trust in the system, as it rules out the need for a central authority or third party to intervene or manipulate the transaction data.

3.4. Types of Blockchains

There are fundamentally three types of blockchains: Public Blockchains, Private Blockchains, and Consortium Blockchains.

Public blockchains are open to anyone. They offer full participant autonomy but require high computational resources and can also have privacy concerns because anyone can see the transactions. Bitcoin and Ethereum are typical examples of public blockchains.

Private blockchains restrict participation and are usually deployed by businesses for proprietary operations. They offer faster and more efficient transactions. However, they sacrifice decentralization.

Consortium blockchains are semi-decentralized and operate under the leadership of a group. They gain the privacy advantages of private blockchains while maintaining certain level of decentralization. They are primarily used in the banking sector.

3.5. Smart Contracts: Automating Transactions

Smart contracts are self-executing contracts with the terms of the agreement directly written into code. They offer automation, autonomy, trust, backup, savings, speed and accuracy. The benefits they offer have driven their increased adaptation across a variety of sectors.

3.6. Blockchain and Cross-border Transactions

Blockchains have the potential to greatly transform the way international transactions occur. They offer several advantages over traditional financial transactions, including transparency, reduced costs, reduced time and increased security.

Understanding these foundational blockchain concepts will set the stage for further discussion about the impact that blockchain technology is having on cross-border payments and international banking. Having delved into this simple guide, these benefits and disruptions should now be easier to see and understand.

Chapter 4. The Cross-Border Challenge: An Overview

The current structure and dynamics of cross-border payments are largely dictated by deeply entrenched systems which have been in operation for many decades. These systems, while reliable, are often characterized by inefficiency, high transaction cost, and a lack of transparency.

4.1. The Traditional Approach

Up until recently, the "correspondent banking" model has been the backbone of the international money transfer system. This model is a network of relationships between large banks spread throughout the world. Essentially, a bank in country A would hold an account with a correspondent bank in country B, and vice versa. This reciprocal relationship allows funds to be transferred securely and reliably between countries.

This decades-old method, while effective, has many drawbacks. It is often time-consuming, given that multiple banks might be involved in a single transaction, each requiring its own processing time. It is also costly; each bank involved typically charges fees for its services. There is also a common criticism of the lack of transparency, as it may be unclear exactly how much the fee will be until it is deducted from the transaction.

Furthermore, the system is disjointed. Different banks and countries often use different systems and technologies, which may not integrate well with each other. This could result in delays.

4.2. The Introduction of Blockchain

Blockchain technology presents an enormous opportunity to revolutionize cross-border payments. Instead of relying on the traditional banking lattice, transactions are verified by a decentralized network of computers, known as nodes, and are then recorded on a blockchain - a transparent, tamper-proof digital ledger.

This substantially reduces the reliance on intermediary banks, resulting in quicker, cheaper, and more efficient transactions. Additionally, since the transaction history is recorded on the blockchain for all to see, it introduces unprecedented levels of transparency into the system.

4.3. The Deutsche Bank Case

One bank that has already begun to explore the potential of blockchain for cross-border payments is Deutsche Bank. In 2016, they completed a six-month proof of concept project using blockchain technology for cross-border payments. Their findings were overwhelmingly positive - they found that by using blockchain, they could reduce costs, increase efficiency, and provide greater transparency for their customers.

4.4. The Ripple Effect

Ripple, a digital payment protocol that uses blockchain technology, is another example of how antiquated cross-border payment systems are being disrupted. Ripple connects different payment systems together, allowing for instant, direct transfers between parties, regardless of location or currency.

By creating a global network, based on blockchain technology, and connecting this to traditional banking systems, Ripple can facilitate cheap and instant international transactions. This is a huge boon for businesses and individuals who regularly make cross-border payments.

4.5. The Regulatory Hurdle

While the potential benefits of blockchain are enormous, there are significant regulatory challenges to overcome. Governments and financial regulators around the world are grappling with a technology that does not neatly fit into existing categories or frameworks.

Regulation of cross-border payments primarily lies with the individual countries involved, and they have often been slow to adapt to new technologies. Moreover, there are concerns about money laundering and terrorist financing, which are often cited as reasons for caution.

This regulatory hurdle isn't insurmountable, however. With time and cooperation, the existing structures could be updated to accommodate blockchain technology without compromising on security or anti-money laundering controls.

Chapter 5. The Future

The traditional model of cross-border payments is being challenged by blockchain technology. The potential benefits - reduced costs, improved efficiency, increased transparency - are too big to ignore. However, despite the hurdles that still remain - particularly around regulation - it is hard to ignore the impact that blockchain could have on the future of international finance. By revolutionizing the way we think about and execute cross-border payments, blockchain could well herald a new era of borderless banking.

Chapter 6. Blockchain and Its Potential in International Transactions

In the borderless world of banking, blockchain technology stands out as an innovative solution capable of transforming international transactions. It is predicted to drive a new era of secure and efficient global payment systems, solving numerous issues that traditional methods have failed to address adequately.

6.1. Understanding Blockchain: A Basic Primer

A blockchain is an immutable and transparent digital ledger that records transactions across multiple computers to ensure the integrity and security. Each 'block' in the chain contains a list of transactions. When a new transaction occurs, it is added to the participant's ledger. Once verified, a new block containing this transaction is attached to the chain, ensuring all records remain linked and accessible.

Blockchain is decentralized, meaning no central authority verifies or manages the transactions. Instead, validation is done through complex algorithms that ensure the security and legitimacy of transactions, making it nearly impossible to alter a record once it's added to the chain.

6.2. Blockchain's Advantages in International Transactions

Blockchain technology promises numerous advantages over

traditional banking in the realm of international transactions. Let's take a look at some of them.

6.3. Enhanced Security

Global transactions involve significant security risks, such as financial fraud, double spending, and cyber threats. Blockchain provides an extra layer of security with its immutable nature – once a transaction is recorded, it cannot be altered, providing optimal protection against fraud. The cryptographic algorithm ensures the transaction identity and authenticity, adding an extra layer of protection.

6.4. Increased Speed

Traditional banking methods often take several days to finalize a cross-border payment, involving multiple intermediaries and various currency exchanges. In contrast, blockchain transactions can be completed almost in real-time, providing significant advantages to businesses and customers alike.

6.5. Reduced Costs

High transfer fees are a common complaint with conventional banking transactions, more so for international ones. Blockchain eliminates the need for intermediaries or third parties, reducing costs associated with their fees. The end user benefits from these reduced costs, making cross-border transactions affordable.

6.6. Transparency and Trust

The transparent and immutable nature of blockchain ensures a high degree of trust amongst participants. All transactions are visible to everyone in the network, ensuring accountability and preventing any unauthorized changes.

6.7. Blockchain in Action: Case Studies

Several financial institutions have recognized the potential of blockchain for international transactions.

6.8. Case Study: Ripple

San Francisco-based start-up Ripple developed a payment protocol that utilizes distributed ledger technology for real-time international transactions. Ripple's XRP token serves as a bridge currency, eliminating the need for multiple currency exchanges and offering faster and more affordable money transfers.

6.9. Case Study: IBM Blockchain World Wire

The IBM Blockchain World Wire (BWW) uses Stellar's protocol for instantaneous clearing and settlement for cross-border payments. It's designed to integrate with existing payment systems, making it a promising tool for institutions looking to adopt blockchain technology.

6.10. Concluding Remarks: The Future of Blockchain in International Transactions

Constant technological development is decreasing the inhibitions and challenges related to implementing blockchain for cross-border payments. As more companies start incorporating distributed ledger technology into their operations, the effects on international transactions will be profound.

Though in its infancy, blockchain's potential in advancing international transactions cannot be overlooked. With its promise for speed, transparency, security, and reduced cost, it is easy to see why it could be the future of global banking. With due time, expansive research, and proper regulation, blockchain technology can bring about a revolution in the banking industry.

Shaping a financial landscape that is less restricted by borders demands vision, and the maturity to navigate the many challenges that are bound to emerge in this transformative journey. Blockchain is undoubtedly a major part of this picture, offering unprecedented opportunities to reshape the way we perform and perceive cross-border transactions. As we continue to explore and experiment with this technology, the next chapter of global finance is being written, paving the way to a truly borderless future.

Chapter 7. The Mechanics of Blockchain in Cross-Border Payments

The advent of blockchain technology has significantly altered the landscape of cross-border payments, paving the way for faster, cheaper, and more secure financial transactions. This development is primarily due to the unique properties and mechanisms inherent in blockchain technology.

7.1. The Basic Principle of Blockchain

Using blockchain for cross-border payments begins with an understanding of the basic structure and principles of blockchain technology.

At the heart of blockchain technology is a publicly available, decentralized database, often referred to as the 'ledger.' This ledger records all transactions made within the system, with each transaction referred to as a 'block.' These blocks are linked together in a chronological sequence to form a 'chain,' hence the name - 'blockchain.'

This method of record-keeping provides robust security structures making it extremely difficult for fraudsters to alter any logged transactions. Each block contains the details of the transaction, such as sender, receiver, value, and timestamp, and most importantly, a unique identifier called the 'hash.' The hash serves as a block's digital fingerprint and is created from the transaction details using a cryptographic function. Each block also contains the hash of the previous block in the chain, creating an unbreakable and verifiable link.

7.2. Applying Blockchain to Cross-Border Payments

In the context of cross-border payments, blockchain offers an innovative alternative to traditional financial systems — a borderless and frictionless transaction environment. Here, financial institutions adopt the role of nodes within the blockchain network. Every time a user initiates a cross-border payment, it is represented as a transaction block which is broadcasted to all nodes in the network.

The role of nodes (financial institutions) is to validate these transactions. Once a certain number of nodes verify the transaction, it becomes a part of the blockchain permanently. This process ensures decentralization, transparency, and security in cross-border payments.

Blockchain also eliminates intermediaries from cross-border payments, reducing fees and processing time. Traditionally, a transfer from Country A to Country B had to pass through various intermediary banks leading to delays and extra costs. With blockchain, the sender can directly transfer to the receiver, via their respective financial institutions, within moments.

7.3. Blockchain's Transformative Features for Cross-Border Payments

Blockchain technology offers many benefits in cross-border transactions, primarily in terms of cost, speed, and transparency.

Cost Efficiency: Blockchain eliminates the need for intermediaries, reducing transaction fees. It can also handle currency conversion, removing an extra layer of cost.

Speed: Traditional cross-border payments can take up to several days to process. However, blockchain can settle transactions in near real-time, sometimes within a few seconds.

Transparency: The distributed nature of blockchain enables users and institutions to track transactions easily. Each transaction block carries all necessary information relevant to the transaction and can be accessed by any party with the necessary permissions.

7.4. The Rise of Digital Currencies in Cross-Border Payments

One of the most interesting developments in cross-border payments via blockchain is the rise of digital or cryptocurrencies. Cryptocurrencies like Bitcoin, Ethereum, and Ripple have grown immensely popular, not only as investment options but also as credible mediums of exchange for cross-border transactions.

Cryptocurrencies serve as both a vehicle of transfer and a store of value. When a sender in Country A wants to send money to a recipient in Country B, they can convert their local currency into a cryptocurrency via a blockchain-based exchange. The cryptocurrency is then sent across the blockchain network, which the recipient in Country B can convert back into their local currency. This method can be faster and cheaper than traditional cross-border systems, and it mitigates currency exchange rate risks, as the conversion is instantaneous.

In conclusion, the impact of blockchain technology on cross-border payments is significant. It empowers businesses and customers with fast, secure and cost-effective transactions, fostering a new era of global financial inclusion. It is, however, a rapidly evolving space that demands regular monitoring, as it continues to face regulatory challenges and issues related to scalability and security. Nonetheless, the possibilities it opens for a truly global, decentralized financial system are undeniably exciting.

Chapter 8. Real World Applications and Case Studies in Blockchain Banking

As we delve into the uncharted territories of blockchain integration in the banking sector, it's vital to ground these pioneering concepts in tangible, relatable case studies. These real-world applications serve as practical examples of the technology's potential, offering a lens through which we can view blockchain's transformative imprint on banking.

8.1. Use Case 1: Cross-Border Payments

Blockchain's potential to revolutionize cross-border payments is entirely grounded in its practical application. A significant case in this aspect is the partnership between Santander, one of the largest banks in Europe, and Ripple, the blockchain payment protocol. Santander's One Pay FX service, powered by Ripple's xCurrent - a real-time settlement system, allows for instant, low-cost international money transfers. This blockchain solution addresses several pain points of traditional banking like slow transaction speeds, high costs, and lack of transparency. Not only has this improved customer satisfaction, but it also positioned Santander as a front-runner in financial innovation.

8.2. Use Case 2: Syndicate Loans

Blockchain technology introduces a level of efficiency previously unseen in the syndicated loans market. A case in point is the Spanish banking group, BBVA. In April 2018, the bank successfully completed a pilot of a blockchain-based syndicated loan amounting to $150 million, involving France's BNP Paribas and Japan's MUFG. This pilot demonstrated the ability of blockchain to shorten loan settlement times from weeks to just a few days, while enhancing transparency and compliance. The success of BBVA's pilot program has significant implications for streamlining complex syndicated loan processes, infusing efficiency, and transparency into a traditionally opaque system.

8.3. Use Case 3: Trade Finance

Trade finance, noted for its paper-intensive processes, has been a focus area for blockchain implementation. The HSBC-ING Bank partnership presented the first scalable live trade finance transaction using blockchain technology. A cargo shipment from Argentina to Malaysia was tracked and processed on a single shared digital application rather than multiple systems, reducing the time for exchange of export documentation from 5-10 days to just 24 hours. This use case accentuates how blockchain can speed up and simplify trade finance operations while reducing costs and risk.

8.4. Use Case 4: Identity Verification

Banks spend significant resources verifying the identity of their clients. Blockchain technology brings forth applications that can drastically reduce the cost and complexity of this process. A noteworthy implementation is BankID, a Norwegian identity verification solution based on blockchain technology. This system is used by all major banks in Norway, allowing customers to authenticate and verify their identity using digital signatures. It's a vital tool for combating identity theft and fraud, and serves as an example of potential blockchain use in the field of identity verification.

8.5. Use Case 5: Regulatory Compliance and Audit

Blockchain technology promises a robust solution for improving regulatory compliance and auditing processes. Estonia's e-Residency program, underpinned by blockchain, provides transparent and secure digital identities. The blockchain-based system allows the government to track and audit transactions, combating the risks of fraud and money laundering. This case study offers a glimpse into how blockchain could redefine regulatory compliance, making it a more transparent, efficient, and secure process.

These examples encapsulate some of the significant applications of blockchain technology in the banking industry. They highlight how the integration of blockchain can address long-standing inefficiencies, reduce costs, and improve transparency. They also provoke further thinking on other potential areas banking can benefit from this dynamic technology.

The realm of blockchain banking continues to evolve, offering unprecedented possibilities. As explored in these case studies, the use of blockchain is more than just speculative theory; it's a practical solution reshaping the contours of global finance. With an understanding of these real-world applications, one can truly comprehend the transformative potential of blockchain banking.

Chapter 9. Future Projections: The Virtual Evolution of Banks

Financial transactions are witnessing a radical shift with the advent of advanced digital technologies. Decades ago, the entire idea of banking was deeply rooted in brick-and-mortar infrastructures. Today, traditional banking services are transforming virtually, becoming more inclusive and extensive - thanks to Blockchain.

9.1. Transition from Traditional to Virtual Banks

As we explored the landscape of traditional banking, we cannot ignore the mountainous pile of paperwork, compliance requirements, and operational inefficiencies that come attached. Delays in transactions, particularly in international transfers, are a common shortcoming. The remittance cost further tallies up, making the experience inconvenient and expensive for the user. Herein, enters the revolutionary crypto-technology - Blockchain.

Blockchain is not just a technology; it is a shift in paradigm that is facilitating the virtual evolution of banks. One of its hallmarks - decentralization - eliminates the need for a central authoritative figure, fueling swift and secure transactions. The virtual banks backed by blockchain technology possess an upper-hand in terms of flexibility, transparency, transaction time, and cost.

9.2. The Emergence of Virtual Banks

Banking on Blockchain doesn't stop at borderless transfers; it expands its wings to include various banking functions in its scope. Loans, savings, investments, insurance, thereby forming the term 'decentralized finance' (DeFi), are also opening up.

Imagine being able to apply for a loan without the need for an intermediary or taking weeks for approval. The blockchain-based smart contracts make this entirely possible. By defining the terms of the agreement based on code and executing them once the predefined conditions are met, smart contracts automate and streamline the process. As well as removing manual interventions, it also minimizes the risk of fraudulent activities, taking banking to an all-new level of security and efficiency.

9.3. Future Projections for Virtual Banks

One might ask, what's in store for the future of virtual banks?

Many industry experts speculate that blockchain technology will become a staple in financial transactions. Be it in the facilitation of immediate settlements, data sharing, fraud reduction, or customer identity verification, blockchain technology will permeate all these realms.

Moreover, as technology continues to advance, we can expect the rise of AI-powered virtual banking assistants, further enhancing the user experience in financial management. These digital assistants may streamline financial planning, offer personalized investment advice, automate bill payments, and much more. With an integrated, AI-based, customer-centric approach, banking will not just be a necessity but a convenient, personalized experience.

9.4. Challenges for Blockchain-Backed Banks

While the potential of blockchain in banking is indeed remarkable, it doesn't come without challenges. Regulatory issues, lack of standardization, scalability, and interoperability are barriers that impede its mainstream adoption. Moreover, the nascent stage of blockchain development means evolving issues such as potential security vulnerabilities would need constant vigilance and improvement.

However, these challenges also present an opportunity. The need for enhanced blockchain technology may lead to the emergence of third-generation decentralized platforms, hyperledger fabric, and Corda technologies.

9.5. Conclusion: Adapting the Banks for Future

The virtual evolution of banks is not an overnight process; it is a journey that requires continuous research, development, and adaptability in response to emerging risks and challenges. While blockchain promises to transform banking, understanding and bridging the gap of its limitations is crucial.

Far from being a novelty, the virtual evolution of banking is a necessity in the rapidly digitizing world. The financial world must adapt or risk obsolescence. Indeed, the harmonious blend of blockchain and banking is set to unlock a world of endless possibilities. As we conclude this chapter, we understand that the future of banking lies in the virtual banks' evolution that harnesses the power of blockchain to its advantage. As we stride forward, we couldn't be more excited about the future that awaits.

Chapter 10. Risk and Regulatory Concerns in Borderless Banking

For every significant technological breakthrough, there is bound to be an assortment of risks and regulatory concerns. Blockchain-based borderless banking is no exception. While the promise of faster, cheaper, and more efficient international transactions is exciting, it is crucial to recognize and navigate the potential pitfalls it presents. These complexities, although challenging, provide ripe opportunities for comprehensive risk management strategies and regulatory adaptations, primed to evolve with the technology.

10.1. The Landscape of Risks

The risks associated with cross-border payments through blockchain are multilayered and can be categorized into operational, financial, and security risks.

Operational risks encompass technology infrastructure, human errors, and inefficiencies. It is essential to put in place fail-safe systems as a safeguard against these risks.

Financial risks include volatility in cryptocurrency values, which can lead to major swings in transaction values between initiation and completion. This risk underlines the need for a robust financial framework that can stabilize prices and safeguard against potential losses.

Security risks encompass potential cyber threats and fraudulent activities. The inherent security features of blockchain technology can significantly lower these risks. However, it is equally crucial to establish a robust security infrastructure to deter any malicious entities.

10.2. The Regulatory Quandary

Cross-jurisdictional transactions raise several regulatory concerns. Regulation becomes complicated due to the differences between national laws and the lack of a central authority in blockchain transactions. Hence, regulators must balance requirements for transparency and accountability with the need for innovation and intellectual property protection.

For blockchain-based cross-border payments to become mainstream, a harmonized international regulatory framework is necessary. This is easier said than done, however, given the varied legal and regulatory environments across the globe. It is imperative to work towards a standardized regulation that respects the sovereignty and jurisdiction of all participating nations while ensuring overall systemic stability.

10.3. Developing a Risk Management Framework

Successful risk management in borderless banking through blockchain requires an understanding of the unique nature of the risks involved and the creation of novel risk frameworks to address these issues.

A successful risk management framework should include specific measures to combat operational, financial, and security risks. It should also sufficiently flexible to adapt to future risks that might emerge as the technology and adoption rates evolve.

The framework should consider four pillars: risk identification, risk assessment, risk mitigation, and risk monitoring and reporting. It's crucial for these pillars to be constantly updated and reviewed for relevance and effectiveness.

10.4. Adapting Existing Regulations

Adapting existing regulations to meet the unique challenges of blockchain-powered borderless banking is a complex task. Some avenues could include creating a regulatory sandbox environment to facilitate experimentation with minimal risk and enabling the interplay of technology with regulation through regulatory technologies (RegTech).

It's equally essential for the development of regulations to keep pace with technology. Regulatory bodies should strive to bridge the gap between the often slower pace of regulation and the quick evolution of technology.

10.5. Final Thoughts

The challenges and risks associated with blockchain-based cross-border payments are complex but not insurmountable. By effectively understanding these risks and framing comprehensive risk management strategies, practitioners can fortify the technology against these potential pitfalls.

On the regulatory front, international cooperation, innovation, and dynamism are key to ensuring a harmonized and conducive environment for the thriving of this technology. Unifying global regulations without stifling the sovereignty and autonomy of individual nations is the need of the hour.

In conclusion, the journey towards the widespread adoption of borderless banking via blockchain may be fraught with challenges, but the potential upside makes the journey worth undertaking. By appropriately managing risks and addressing regulatory concerns, we can unlock an exciting future where boundaries indeed become a thing of the past.

Chapter 11. Investment Opportunities in Blockchain Technology

Blockchain technology, one of the greatest breakthroughs in the digital age, brings forth various opportunities that could prove profitable for investors. While it started as a technology to support the cryptocurrencies, it has grown into a versatile platform that offers a myriad of advantages spanning different sectors, including the financial industry.

11.1. Understanding Blockchain Technology

To appreciate the investment opportunities this tech presents, one must first grasp the fundamentals of the technology. Blockchain technology could best be understood as a decentralized ledger of all transactions across a peer-to-peer network. This ledger's decentralization ensures its invulnerability against tampering, fraud, and interference. Once the information has been recorded, its irreversible nature makes blockchain apt for recording events, titles, agreements, transactions, and other essential information.

Blockchain technology provides transparency, reducing fraud in financial transactions. Its decentralized nature dispenses the need for a third party, thus eliminating associated costs and enhancing efficiency. Blockchain technology also enables secure, fast transactions, and is expected to dramatically reduce the cost of transacting while increasing transaction speed.

11.2. Blockchain as a Disruption in Finance

The finance industry stands as one of the leading fields ripe for blockchain disruption, hence the immense interest from investors. Blockchain could drastically augment the efficiency of transactions in financial services. It stands at a potential crossroads of the traditional financial system providing a decentralized solution for payments, remittances, savings, insurance, lending and securities trading. This includes emerging trends such as DeFi (Decentralized Finance) which aims to substitute traditional financial intermediaries.

Several financial companies and institutions are investing heavily in research and development projects involving the blockchain. These investments cite reducing operational costs, improving transaction speed, security, and improved customer experience as the main factors influencing their decisions. This level of interest from established finance sector players further authenticates the potential and validity of blockchain technology.

11.3. Investing in Blockchain Startups

Startup companies focusing on blockchain technology provide a significant investment opportunity. These startups range from those that provide blockchain technology infrastructures to those that use it to provide new kinds of services. Investors can approach them directly or indirectly by supporting enterprises that invest in blockchain startups.

11.4. Blockchain-based Products and Services

Companies using blockchain to provide products and services offer another zone for investment. For instance, blockchain is revolutionizing supply chain management by providing real-time, unalterable records. Such companies offer investors a growth-oriented prospect as they harness the blockchain's power to drive operational efficiencies.

Due to the unique nature of each entity, it is crucial to review the company's business model, the potential market size it is targeting, the management team, and its financial health before investing.

11.5. Cryptocurrency as an Investment Option

The creation of the blockchain technology paved the way for the first cryptocurrency, Bitcoin. Today, there are thousands of different cryptocurrencies that operate on the blockchain, providing an array of investment opportunities. The inherent volatility within the crypto markets can offer significant returns but also presents large risks.

Cryptocurrency investments come in numerous forms. An investor can buy the coins directly and gain from any increase in value or invest in crypto mining where new coins are rewarded. There's also an opportunity to invest in companies providing infrastructure services, such as crypto exchanges, wallets, and payment services.

11.6. Initial Coin Offerings (ICOs)

An ICO is an event where a new cryptocurrency project sells part of its cryptocurrency tokens to early adopters in exchange for payment in an immediate, liquid value token like Bitcoin or Ether. It's akin to an initial public offering (IPO) where a private company decides to go public and sell its shares to institutional or accredited investors. However, ICOs have been much maligned due to widespread fraud and regulatory non-compliance, caution is explicitly advised.

11.7. Making Wise Blockchain Investment Decisions

Blockchain investments should not be made lightly, as with any investment, a high level of due diligence is required. Before investing in any blockchain-related opportunity, take the time to understand the underlying technology. This will help you understand the potential and limitations of the investments you are considering. Furthermore, the rapidly evolving nature of blockchain technology means that investors must maintain a long-term perspective.

In summary, the blockchain is likely to disrupt several major industries, which could create numerous investment opportunities. Through understanding, vigilance and a long-term perspective, you can wisely exploit the potential benefits of these changing dynamics for successful blockchain investment decisions.

Chapter 12. The Road to a Borderless Financial Future

Globalization and technology have pushed us to the cusp of significant developments in international finance, with cross-border transactions serving as a pivotal facet. This progress has been fueled by the interplay between traditional banking institutions, blockchain technology, and the evolving landscape of international payments. Our comprehensive exploration of this journey begins now, illuminating the pathway towards a borderless financial future.

12.1. The Evolution of Cross-Border Transactions

Cross-border transactions have been a vital part of global commerce even before the dawn of organized banking. Coins of different weights and metals were transported cross-border and used as the medium of exchange between civilizations. Over centuries, the mechanisms evolved and matured; letters of credit in the Middle Ages, establishment of central banks during Renaissance, and the gold standard introduced in the nineteenth century, paving the way to modern international banking.

In the past few decades, however, the nature of cross-border transactions has undergone another paradigm shift. The introduction of swift codes and electronic money transfers in the 1970s streamlined international payments and reduced transfer time significantly. However, the system remained expensive, exclusionary, and heavily dependent on a handful of large banking corporations globally. Every transaction passed through multiple intermediaries, each taking its share of fees and time.

But the advent of the 21st century marked the beginning of a technological revolution that promised to upend these traditional and deeply entrenched mechanisms.

12.2. Blockchain: A Disruptive Force

When the mysterious figure of Satoshi Nakamoto introduced Bitcoin in 2009, it was not just a new form of digital currency that was presented to the world, but also the revolutionary technology that powered it – the blockchain. As open, distributed ledger systems, blockchains promise transparency, traceability, and security while cutting out intermediaries. It didn't take long for innovators to see the potential for using blockchains beyond cryptocurrencies and apply it to cross-border transactions.

In a blockchain-powered cross-border transaction, traditional banking intermediaries are made redundant. Instead, the transaction amount in the sender's currency is converted into a digital token on one end, transferred across the distributed ledger, and then converted back into the receiver's currency at the other end. This process drastically reduces the number of steps involved in traditional money transfers, increases the speed of transactions, and brings down costs.

Yet, blockchains also face significant hurdles. Widespread understanding and acceptance of the technology are as yet limited. Additionally, governments and regulatory bodies around the world are still grappling with how to classify, regulate, and tax transactions carried out through blockchain.

12.3. The Revolution in Cross-Border Payments

Even as blockchain technology continues to evolve, it has already started transforming cross-border payment systems. Ripple, a prominent player in this space, collaborates with banks and other financial institutions worldwide to offer a global cross-border payment system powered by its blockchain-based platform.

Ripple's system allows cross-border transactions to take place in seconds, and at significantly lower costs than traditional SWIFT-based systems. However, while Ripple's payment system does involve digital currencies (XRP), it also enables transactions in traditional fiat currencies. This demonstrates the potential for blockchain technology to revolutionize cross-border transactions without completely abandoning fiat currencies.

At the same time, cryptocurrencies themselves are becoming an increasingly popular medium for cross-border transactions. Companies like BitPay are enabling businesses across the world to accept payments in Bitcoin and other digital currencies, thus opening up new possibilities for international trade.

12.4. The Challenges Ahead

As we stand at the brink of this financial revolution, paths to a borderless financial future remain fraught with challenges. Regulatory hurdles, technological glitches, scaling issues, and concerns surrounding cybersecurity are all significant barriers that can impede progress.

Moreover, the transformation of the banking system won't happen overnight. Traditional banking institutions have been deeply ingrained in our economic infrastructures for centuries. Shifting towards a blockchain-based system, therefore, will take time and a significant amount of strategic planning and execution.

12.5. Conclusion: The Road Ahead

Embracing blockchain technology for cross-border transactions is not just about speeding up transfers or reducing costs. It's about creating a fairer, more inclusive global financial system. The promised land of a borderless financial future isn't simply about the absence of physical or geographical borders; it's about tearing down the economic barriers that exclude billions around the world from accessing basic financial services.

As the world adjusts to this revolutionary technology, the road towards a borderless financial future will, undoubtedly, be little less than a roller coaster ride. Yet, the potential benefits that lie at the end of this journey make it an extremely exciting, albeit challenging, one.

Externally-powered momentum paired with internal adoption and innovation will continue to push this frontier. One thing is clear - the banking of tomorrow will be vastly different, borderless, and we have front-row seats to this remarkable transformation.